ABANDONED DETROIT
VACANT SCHOOLS

TONY VIENNEAU

America Through Time is an imprint of Fonthill Media LLC
www.through-time.com
office@through-time.com

Published by Arcadia Publishing by arrangement with Fonthill Media LLC
For all general information, please contact Arcadia Publishing:
Telephone: 843-853-2070
Fax: 843-853-0044
E-mail: sales@arcadiapublishing.com
For customer service and orders:
Toll-Free 1-888-313-2665

www.arcadiapublishing.com

First published 2019

Copyright © Tony Vienneau 2019

ISBN 978-1-63499-158-2

Typeset in Trade Gothic 10pt on 15pt
Printed and bound in England

CONTENTS

ABOUT THE AUTHOR

TONY VIENNEAU is a local Detroit photographer and videographer. He has always been interested in history and has a spirit for adventure. From an early age, he was trying to travel and find interesting and fun places in the Detroit area to explore. After he took interest in photography, he began his career of uncovering and documenting abandoned buildings throughout Michigan. His work also included videography through his media group named Detroit Exploration, which focused mainly on filming cinematic and detailed video throughout these vacant buildings. After the success of his work in Detroit, Tony began traveling America to broaden his collection of abandoned photography.

INTRODUCTION

From an early age, I was always interested in vacant buildings throughout Detroit. Seeing them on the side of the road left me with so many questions. There was something so intriguing about peering through those broken glass windows. Just admiring them from the outside was never enough for me—I wanted to dig deeper. Curiosity eventually got the best of me when I planned my first trip. As I researched these places and uncovered their history, I immediately fell in love with abandonment. Linking with the community and meeting so many inspired people was a huge motivator for me. Stepping foot inside my first abandoned building was invigorating. Heart racing, adrenaline flowing, I did not know what I was expecting on the other side of that door.

Little did I know, behind those walls is a glorious hidden paradise. Documents and items left behind tell an extremely powerful story. Some buildings are completely gutted and left prone to structural damage and collapse, while others decay naturally with fields of green moss and thick vegetation.

Preservation is the most important aspect of the hobby. Nothing is worse than finding a building vandalized or scrapped completely. These are important pieces of history and they need to be treated with respect. You constantly hear the phrase, "Take nothing but photos and leave nothing but footsteps." This is the testament most of us keep close to the heart. What we do is not destructive, and I am constantly informing people outside of the hobby that I am an artist and not a vandal. It can be dangerous at times, but I am willing to temporarily sacrifice my own safety for a beautiful photograph or a story to tell later. I am always trying to show off the hidden beauty the other side has to offer. Abandoned photography just feels right and it's what keeps me passionate. The excitement I receive from finding new locations to document is a feeling I cannot describe. I feel the story my photography tells is crucial, showing off a part of Detroit most people would never see. I am incredibly fortunate to be able to share my story and I hope to inspire many to discover beauty in everything. If I've inspired just one person at the end of the day, my journey was well worth it.

1

BARBOUR MAGNET MIDDLE SCHOOL

Abandonment knows no bounds; a statement that is especially true in Detroit. Beautiful and intricate facades sit dormant overlooking Detroit's once beautiful neighborhoods. Street corners that students once stood on to catch the bus or gather after school are now unrecognizable due to thick overgrowth and grime. Even the most prestigious schools are no match for a crumbling economy and massive population decrease, and Barbour Magnet Middle School was unfortunately no exception.

Metal security panels bolted to the outside of a classroom window.

When I stumble upon Barbour, I have to stand back and appreciate it for a while. The façade seems to stretch through the clouds around this crowded suburb. Narrow streets and tightly spaced homes make this school seem more like a castle, with the perimeter fence around it standing as a mote to deter any possible intruders. Barbour's central brass tower, still standing tall, is a true staple of Detroit Public Schools' infrastructure. Most of the glistening glass of the windows are intact, a real oddity for this area. Detailed faces and statues etched above entryways and center points throughout its historic exterior keep a watchful eye.

Entering the school, I am certainly not disappointed. Hallways stretch as far as the eye can see littered with paint flakes and metal pipes protruding from the ornate ceiling above. Lockers once crammed full of books and school supplies are now beginning to rust away and shed their vivid colors. I notice something extremely interesting while I traverse to the second floor: several different layers of paint peeling and showing themselves. Each layer of paint telling its own story throughout time, each step I take crunching away at the history.

A drinking fountain pulled out in the middle of the hallway to be scrapped.

Custodian's closet with creepy glossed window panes.

Lockers proudly presenting years of flaking paint.

A landing in one of the three main staircases.

A look from the running track down onto one of the gym floors.

Ascending through the empty floors, I am surprised to find something rarely seen—two separate gymnasiums. Both gyms are identical with a center corridor connecting them. Hanging idly is a thick climbing rope attached to the rafters. It's truly amazing to see floors shiny enough to cast a reflection and basketball nets completely intact. The wood floors rise several feet from water damage, stretching like bright waves in the ocean.

Taking two steps out from the gymnasium, I see something that really catches my eye: the most glorious library. Positioned in the dead center of the school, it proudly shows off the slick wood panels and detailed celling trim. A large front desk sits elegantly at the front of the room, its countertops now dusted with paint flakes and ceiling dust. Lining the top of the library walls are portraits and paintings tucked behind clear plastic covers.

The library front desk surrounded by beautiful wood pillars.

Notes still scribbled on a classroom chalkboard.

Each classroom has such charm to it. Passing from room to room, I notice they are individually colored to give them some character. Chalk boards still have notes scribbled across them from previous lessons and classroom decorations hang sadly across pinup boards. The students and staff who attended likely did not know what the future had for their historic middle school.

2

CADILLAC MIDDLE SCHOOL

A question commonly asked is how the neighbors feel about me creeping through these vacant buildings. Surprisingly enough, neighbors really don't mind once they realize I'm only there for documenting and research purposes. Of course, every few times I go out, I'm faced with a curious neighbor or two coming out to question me. This always allows me to hear some history and background of the neighborhood from people who grew up there and have experienced the decline in their school district over time.

The library room surrounded by metal security shutters.

One set of stories from an elderly man I met during my first visit to Cadillac Middle School stuck with me. As I approach the building, I hear a man call out to me from his house. Turning around, I see he is making his way toward me from the porch. As he gets closer, I can see his eyes light up when he notices my camera gear. The man begins explaining that he has been living in the same home for over fifty years. He recalls all the fun he had when he attended the school and remembers every detail inside and out: gym class and math tests and just about everything in between. A wave of sadness suddenly hits us both as we stand admiring the decaying façade of this piece of history. This man had seen the school through its prime and witnessed its heart-breaking downfall. His neighborhood was falling apart around him and it was completely out of his control.

Central hallway outside of the front office of the school.

Empty gym and cafeteria with all the nets fully intact.

One of the upper-floor hallways decorated in bright blue paint.

Balancing on an overturned filing cabinet, I slowly descend into the school. Watching my foot placement is very important as I drop down into the belly of the beast—the boiler room. I am immediately blown away by the intricate layout of this place. Thousands of tubes, dials, and wires are all laced together, forming the heart of this school.

Climbing up to the main floor, I am caught off guard by the most amazing cyan colored walls. Ceiling tiles have begun to drop and crumble to the floor from the constantly changing climate. All the windows throughout the halls are covered from the outside by thick metal security shutters, leaving an ominous darkness throughout the empty corridors. Plaques still hang on the walls, showing off sports achievements and staff member of the month awards dating back to the early 90s.

Wall of plaques and awards won by students and staff.

A vacant piano directly outside of the music room.

On the second floor, I find the music room completely gutted of any character besides the flaking silhouettes of famous musicians plastered about. The only thing remaining is a beautiful, old piano collecting dust in the hallway. Just like the rest of the school, this piano sits in disrepair and is completely discarded. These classrooms and hallways that were once packed with thousands of happy students and staff are now left to dark corridors, open for nature to begin its slow takeover.

Decals of famous musicians and music pattern guides.

3

COLIN POWELL ACADEMY

Sometimes the locations I visit massively exceed my expectations. From beautiful architecture to elegant layout, every school I've visited has something that makes it stand out to me. Even the smallest schools have something special to give it character. Colin Powell Academy is an example of a school that is absolutely packed with character and significant history. I can confidently say this school is one of my favorite abandoned places I've ever stepped foot in, and for very good reason.

A comfortable looking chair in one of the empty classrooms.

The thing I notice immediately upon approaching the school is the physical scale of it. The building stretches almost the entire length of the block and rises far into the sky with its distinct three stories. The outside is covered in huge, detailed stone arches around the windows and doors. Almost all the glass is intact in the upper floors and most of the foundation remains in great shape. Overgrowth has taken much of the perimeter and trees crawl across most of the sealed doors.

Walls leading up to the gym still reflecting and shining with the sunlight.

Taking my first step into this building, I am immediately greeted by a large cluttered staircase full of debris and garbage. Climbing up the stairs, I am met by the large open chapel that once brought thousands of students together for prayer. There is a balcony that connects all the way around the chapel, allowing students to view the mass from the second story. In the center of the room is an old electric organ that once created beautiful music, but is now dismantled and destroyed.

Above: Chapel room with a busted-up organ in the center.

Opposite above: Beautiful arch window frames letting in plenty of natural light.

Opposite below: Intricate window decorations and curtains have been ripped from their original mounted positions.

School work and textbooks scattered across the floor.

Walking through the gigantic hallways, I notice that classrooms are still full of books and belongings. Cabinets are still packed with school materials and students' projects. Water logged ceiling tiles coat the ground and squish as I venture deeper through the winding halls. Covering most of the walls is bright yellow tile. These tiles are sparkling in the sunlight as if they had been polished just yesterday. The ground, unfortunately, was dirty and damaged from years of decay and weathering.

One of the main hallways with all the lockers removed.

Finally arriving in the gym, I realize why this school took up so much space on the block. This gym is spectacular and appears to have been built to survive the test of time. Thick orange beams and pillars weave across the ceiling over the basketball court. Steel poles help support a seating area for spectators to view the game from above. In the center is a thick coating of moss and mold created by the cold, damp air of this dungeon.

During the time I was in this building, a storm passed overhead. All throughout the hallways the only thing audible is the drips and drops of the water falling through the cracks that had formed in the collapsing ceiling. Buckets had been set out years prior and tarps were spread out to catch any leaks. Of course, through the years, these preventive measures were of no use. As time ticks on, the water slowly takes its toll and eventually will lead to some serious destruction.

Brightly colored supports stretch across the double gym.

4

COOLIDGE ELEMENTARY SCHOOL

A vast majority of the places I visit are unfortunately not as clean and inviting as I would hope they'd be. A lot of the time these places are completely decimated years before they're even on my radar. Sadly, Coolidge Elementary School is far passed the point of salvation. All that's left is the husk of a building once prospering in Detroit's booming economy.

An inner court yard with views of the shrubs on the bottom floor.

Approaching the front door of the school, I am very unsure of what I'm about to experience. Glass litters the sidewalk and road around the school and thick vegetation tangles most of the outside of the building. Most of the old doors are busted open to expose the true destruction that is being held within. Cheap plywood is fashioned over all the windows, some of which have fallen off from years of storms and wind.

A paper sign still hangs from when the school was operational.

Almost every single ceiling tile has fallen.

From my first steps in, I'm already feeling wary. With the condition of the place, you'd think you were stepping into a haunted house. The hallways are pitch black besides the beams of light leaking in through the damaged boards over the windows. Lockers have been ripped out of the walls and sold for scrap, leaving huge empty holes throughout the bare corridors. The small glass panels that were imbedded in the wooden doors have all been shattered by vandals and now coat the disgusting, damp floor. The floor creaks and shifts under my feet as I move further in.

Gates have been installed on the outside of these windows to prevent them from being busted.

Some windows have been taken out of their frame to prevent them from being damaged.

The classrooms are unrecognizable. Areas on the ceiling that once held beautiful florescent light fixtures are now nothing but empty holes and fixtures have been discarded throughout the empty rooms. Wooden floor boards have begun to warp and crack from the moisture and leave each room with a thick, musty stench. What's left of the shattered windows is now protected by crude wooden barricades affixed from the outside. Shelves and closets that once contained teachers' class materials have deteriorated into warped and cracking pieces of wood and debris.

Nothing is left besides doors in this hallway.

Seeing the condition of this school is shocking. It honestly makes you wonder how things like this could have been prevented. This school once had thousands of students and hundreds of teachers walking through its hallways. One day, the doors closed for the very last time and nobody had any idea it would turn out like quite like this. Students had to relocate, staff were completely out of jobs. It's a sad reality, but a common one in Detroit. Each school represents a piece of history that should never be forgotten and the stories they tell are very important. We should never forget the lessons learned from the past because history always repeats itself.

A cleaner upper floor with light peeking through the doorways.

5

DUKE ELLINGTON

One of the biggest threats to these abandoned schools is not natural decay, but human intervention. These buildings are built from the ground up with weather proofing and infrastructure to withstand any storms Detroit could possibly have. Most older schools are still standing double as tornado shelters and even civil defense shelters capable of protecting thousands of students and staff during an attack. Unfortunately, even the toughest schools are no match for arson, scrapping, and excessive vandalism.

A piano is the only thing left in this band room.

After Duke Ellington closed its doors in 2013, it was lightly used by the church right across the street as a community center. Its fate was sealed when a fire broke out in 2016 and burned a majority of its first floor. So much history was lost from this fire and it's very unlikely the property will recover from extensive structural damage. The building's location, so close to a busy intersection and the Detroit City Airport, make it the prime subject for demolition, but only time will tell.

Piles of ash and debris collected in one of the central stairwells.

Much of this hallway is damaged by fire and the ceiling is black from the smoke.

Stepping through the front door to this school is nightmare fuel. The bottom floor, which had been ripped apart from the fire, is left with only the concrete walls and steel beams off the ceiling. Black soot coats every surface that came in contact with the smoke. Remnants of children's text books and toys are thrown about the halls and lockers. Piles of ash and debris are piled up through the classrooms, making each step quite the obstacle.

Children's toys posed and dirty from sitting for so long.

One of the first things I notice upon entering Duke Ellington is its beautiful gym. The gym is in phenomenal condition and doesn't match the school around it. Floors appear to have a certain shine about them as if they have just been waxed. The stage lights that once flooded the auditorium with glorious lights and colors remain perfectly intact. An anti-drug banner hangs on the wall, right of the main stage, proudly announcing its imperative message.

Much of the gym is still intact and there are piles of old equipment and items.

The charred remains of books and students' belongings in cubbies.

Since the school was once utilized by a church, a lot of the classrooms in the basement are full of old pews and furniture. So much equipment is just left behind and forgotten in this school, it's honestly shocking. It's always crushing to see so much time and money invested into places like these, only to burn to the ground. It's a very sad reality in which so much is lost and is unable to be recovered, but regrettably all too common.

Desks are still left throughout most of the classrooms.

6

FOCH HIGH SCHOOL

After a school closes, it is usually secured very quickly and efficiently. Even with huge metal shutters over windows and cameras projecting live video to surveillance companies, sometimes it's just not enough. Scrappers that dig through abandoned buildings and pick out valuable metals and materials are a force nobody can counter. These scrappers will fight and demolish their way into just about any structure imaginable. Schools are often the first places targeted due to their size and abundance of copper and metals that can be easily turned around for cash.

The story behind Foch High School is quite an interesting one. After closing its doors, Detroit Public Schools was quick on the draw with installing some expensive and state-of-the-art camera equipment to protect the high school's halls. The surveillance system protected the school for just a few short years before it was dismantled by scrappers. Although power was not cut to the school, all alarms and security features had been completely disabled and the school was now vulnerable to an onslaught. The floodgates had opened.

Clean hallways littered with ceiling tiles and broken glass.

My first experience coming through the hallways is very unsettling. The hallways are something you would only see in a zombie movie. Half of the lights are damaged and blown out, ballasts left to swing freely above a sea of glass. The lights that are intact flicker and glow dimly. Buzzing of electricity is heard faintly above the ceiling tiles.

Some of the fluorescent lights are still intact and show off a creepy corridor.

A spotless gym with the lights still turned on.

The layout of the halls seems oddly familiar. Two gyms attached with a central library, standing tall in the center. The building architecture is identical to Barbour Middle School as they are sister schools and designed around the same blueprints. It is quite common for the architects to reuse their designs and it makes it especially easy to navigate when I enter these schools.

Sporadic ceiling lights glow inside the library.

The central focus of this school is its glorious auditorium. Rows of dark green seats align perfectly with the ornate ceiling above. Four intricate chandeliers protrude and shine light down onto the tiered seating. Gigantic windows stretch from the floor to the ceiling, illuminating the entire room with warm sunlight. Lime green trim runs along the walls to accent the darker green shown below.

A perfectly preserved auditorium

The classrooms are particularly elegant here. Each room has a different colored wall and eccentric tile work to match. No single room is the same design, giving Foch that extra bit of character. It is slightly unnerving being in an abandoned building with power and TVs left on. Each classroom is filled with an eerie light and sounds of ambient TV static. Each time I step into a different room, I never know what I'm going to be faced with.

Above: Zig-zag tile patterns across one of the classrooms.

Opposite above: Warped wood floors and peeling paint are seen throughout the bottom floor.

Opposite below: A lesson plan is still listed on this chalkboard.

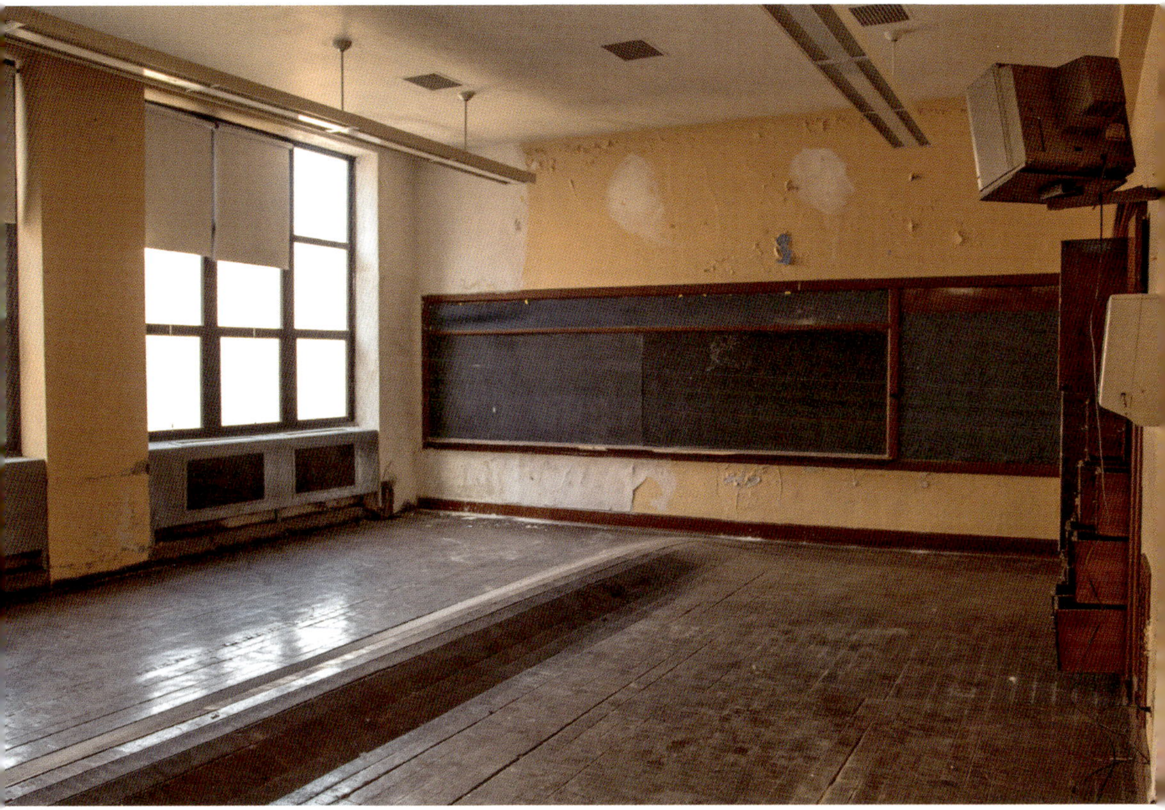

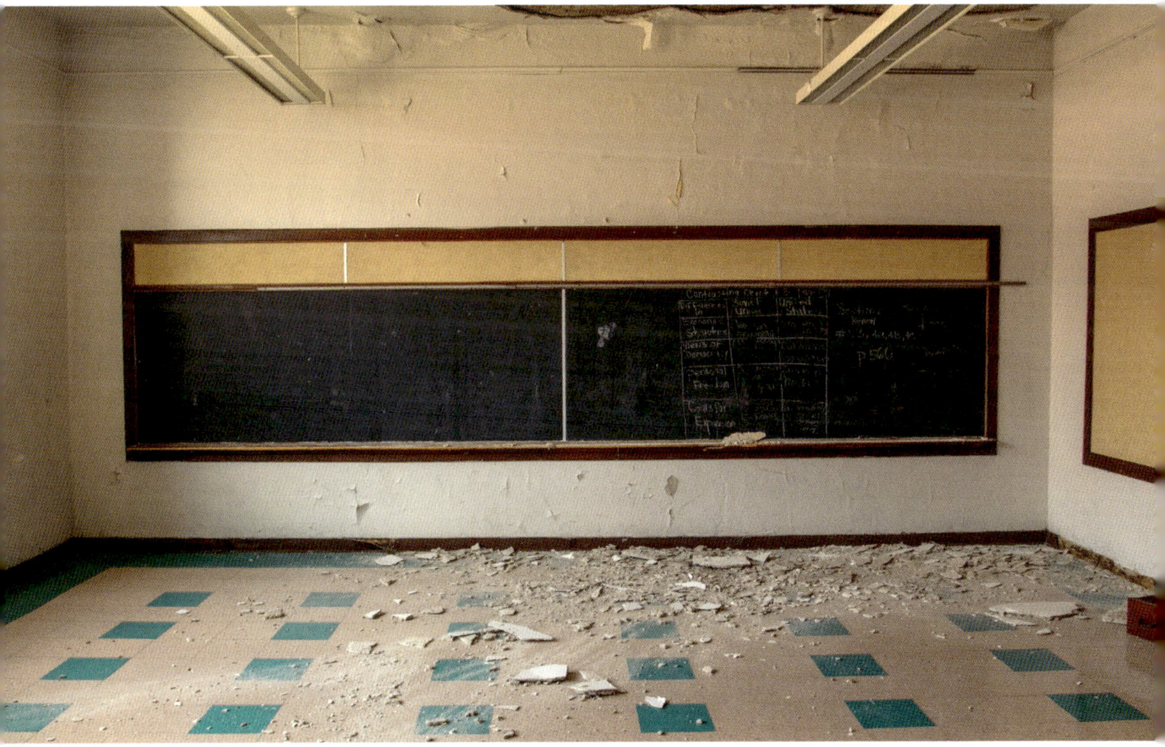

7

HERMAN ELEMENTARY SCHOOL

Occasionally, I have a school in my sights I would like to document that I watch for weeks or even months on end until I'm able to gain access, checking in periodically to see if they're continuing to maintain the property or keep up on security. Some schools are high on my priority and Herman Elementary was one of them. I had been watching Herman for over a year before the electricity was shut off and the first signs of scrapping were shown. As soon as I heard the news of its opening, I was quick to make my way inside. I was one step behind the vandals, but what I documented was well worth the wait.

A storage room decorated with cyan paint on the walls.

My first few steps into this school lead me directly into the gym. The first thing I notice is the floors have no warp to them yet. Generally wooden gym floors like this one will begin to warp from moisture and temperature shifts. My eyes are drawn to the vibrant yellow on the walls—it's hard to look over. Several deflated basketballs sit on the side lines. A long banner still hangs, showing an artistic view of the Detroit city skyline; what a beautiful touch.

Bright yellow walls around a clean gym floor.

The hallways are decorated in the most brilliant colors. Old classroom signs still hang on detailed metal hooks and provide a guide through the maze-like hall system. Most of the classrooms are locked and their door handles have been removed. I am only able to peer in through the window to see what's on the other side. Most of the classrooms are left a mess and a lot of the non-valuable equipment is thrown about and destroyed on the floor. A tattered American flag still hangs proudly in what appears to be a history class. World maps are also left to be vandalized and torn apart.

Above: Classroom signs still hanging above an empty hallway.

Opposite above: A geography class still set up with maps and an American flag hanging above.

Opposite below: A globe sits in the intersection of the main hallways.

ASIA
EAS

204
200B
200A

A game of Jenga on a table surrounded by open textbooks.

The library is spectacular. So much has just been left and thrown throughout the room. Tables still stand covered in various class books. A table is decorated with what appears to be children's building blocks. The floor is covered in a sea of books tossed from the bookshelves. I notice a student's poster board assignment sitting in the corner, proudly sporting a passing grade.

Children's building blocks sprawled over a library table.

The final piece to this beautiful puzzle is the auditorium. I never expect to find an auditorium this put together—it's truly a blessing. A piano is tucked away in front, likely out of tune with most of the keys smashed. The windows let in a beautiful light onto the old wooden seats. The smooth wood panels surrounding the stage are shining as if freshly polished. It is such a shame to see a piece of architectural beauty rot away like this.

A grand auditorium shining brightly.

8

KELSO BRUCE ACADEMY

The early bird gets the worm. This sentiment is particularly true in the world of urban exploring. In this environment, if you're not checking up on these buildings regularly you may never have the chance to view the inside. Even in buildings with freshly locked doors and alarm systems, things can change in a single night. My entrance into Kelso Bruce Academy was a subtle victory and a true example of excellent timing and dedication. What I found when I entered made all my time and effort well worth it.

This classroom was still put together from when the school closed.

I am immediately greeted by a very unwelcoming sound upon entry; alarms. Quickly, I run to the hallway and check the main alarm panel. I let out a huge sigh of relief as I find the alarms are not communicating and the wires have been sliced. It was an odd feeling being in this place with the electricity on and alarms blaring.

Making my way across the main wall, I notice much of the equipment and supplies from the classrooms have been piled up in the hallways. Beautiful multi-colored lockers line the hallways, providing some color and bringing the place to life. The bright yellow walls are something I have never seen before, either, and flow well with the rest of the historic pieces in the school. Even the classrooms are decorated in bright, warm colors around delicate wood accent frames. Some classrooms proudly presented the original decorative fireplaces seldom seen throughout schools in Detroit.

A bright center hallway bursting with color.

One of the decorative fireplaces inside a classroom.

The library is a true relic. Bookshelves are still fully stocked with thousands of old books and chairs are all stacked up in the corner, waiting to be set up once again. The gym is in pristine condition, with nets still hanging and the floors sparkling in the sunlight. The beautiful auditorium has unfortunately been ripped apart and is being used for storage. The kitchen is still in working order, with refrigerators full of expired food and cabinets stocked with pots and pans. All these features are unfortunately not being utilized and sit at the mercy of the Detroit Public School system.

Bookshelves are still full of old books.

CASH FOR KIDS & WNBA DETROIT SHOCK
GYMNASIUM
Cash for Kids
SHOCK

Above: This kitchen has all the equipment and appliances left behind.

Opposite above: Gym floors still sparkling from the fluorescent lights and sunlight.

Opoosite below: The auditorium has been set up as a storage room.

Although Kelso Bruce currently sits in a state of abandonment, the future is looking up for it. The infrastructure is sound, and it has been secured enough to prevent any structural damage. Extensive work is being done to keep up on the facility and I hope this continues. It is a true Detroit gem with a very rich history and should make easy ground for anybody looking to renovate or move in. Moving forward, this spot will always be on my radar and I will be documenting its eventual transformation.

9

KETTERING HIGH SCHOOL

Sometimes in the Detroit Public School system, abandoned schools are closed with very short notice and much of the items inside are left behind. There is really no limit to what you can find inside of some of these places and it isn't uncommon to find valuable equipment or technology left to rot. The reasons why some schools are left in this state are sometimes unknown and really makes you wonder.

Old technology discarded inside of a classroom.

My trip through Kettering high school is shocking and I am truly amazed at the amount of equipment and items left behind. Kettering is much more modern than other schools in its area. There are no frills on the outside and looking at it from the street, it appears just like any other metro Detroit high school. The inside tells a much different story and makes you question what really happened through it's dark and desolate hallways.

The courtyard walls have been torn out, letting in trees and vegetation.

From the first few steps, I notice almost nothing was removed following the closure of the school. Desks are still set up in line and cabinets are crammed with yearbooks and textbooks from previous years. Filing cabinets are broken open, with contents thrown about by vandals and looters. The paint from the ceiling has begun to flake off and coats most of the surfaces through the classrooms. A classroom I stumble upon has all the original cooking and baking equipment used from a previous cooking class. Gigantic ovens are still completely intact and coated with oil and rust from sitting. A heavy stand mixer is also left behind to rust and collect dust. This equipment was likely top of the line when it was implemented but will never receive any further use.

Opposite above: Kettering was one of the few schools that received a full library makeover sponsored by the Detroit Pistons basketball team.

Opposite below: A stand mixer left behind inside of a cooking classroom.

BIOGRAPHY
Individual Biographies
Collective Biographies
Autobiographies
FICTION
Adventure
Science Fiction
Sports
Romance
FICTION
Adventure
Science Fiction
Sports
Romance
FICTION
Adventure
Science Fiction
Sports
Romance
REFERENCE

HOBART

Walking into the auditorium for the first time, I am astonished by the sheer size of it. Hundreds of cloth seats line the auditorium right in front of the massive main stage. The ceiling is lined with metal beams laced in a very intricate pattern. Rays of sunlight peak through small holes busted in the ceiling by scrappers. Right behind the stage curtains is where dance was practiced. A mirror lines the entire length of the room and skylights fill the room up with natural light.

A very large auditorium was created to accommodate a high volume of students.

The signature Kettering sign displayed in the court yard.

All of the glass in the interior of the school has been removed or busted out, leaving vegetation to begin growing into the hallways. Beautiful flowers still bloom even through destruction and decay. The Kettering "K" sign still stands proudly amongst the overgrown shrubs and remnants of an old playground are hidden behind it all. In only a few short years, nature has almost completely engulfed this school.

Even through decay, flowers still begin to bloom.

10

JOHN C MARSHALL ELEMENTARY

They truly don't build them like they used to. I hear this a lot while exploring and I've learned it's particularly true when talking about Detroit's older abandoned schools. Not only are the structures themselves built to last, but the facades and exterior details are phenomenal displays of meticulous craftsmanship. Every school is different and has unique characteristics. The materials they used and the stone work is always breathtaking, and the attention to detail is very apparent.

This is where the kids would line up to get their food for lunch.

John Marshall Elementary is protected like a fortress. Squeezing between the towering castle-like fence into the thick brush of the courtyard feels surreal. Trees tangle together against the bright blue sky and it feels more like a forest than an abandoned school. Trees push past the rooftop and provide natural shade onto the overgrown courtyard. I work my way through the urban jungle into the inviting open window and hop up into the school. I am greeted by the familiar sight of warped wood floors and flaking paint. Although the ceiling tiles have mostly all dropped to the floor, the rest of the school is surprisingly clean.

Spiked fences secure the center courtyard.

Each set of lockers were decorated with a different neon color.

One step into the hallway and I am greeted by the most magnificent colors. Each set of lockers is painted a different neon color brightly reflecting the sunlight peering through the windows. The walls are colored a glorious cyan that catches my eye as I venture further in. Boxes of school supplies and books still pile up outside the classrooms. Almost all desks and equipment have been removed either by scrappers or the school district, leaving classrooms empty. A large intricate fountain stands proudly near the main office, with tiles dusty and damaged.

A decorative tile fountain in the front of the main office.

Cinder blocks have fallen through certain areas of the ceiling on the top floor.

    As I climb to the second floor, things start to get shaky. Much of the roof has begun to take damage from the elements. Huge cinder blocks from the roof have come crashing through into one of the classrooms; nature is a terrifying force. Through the hallways I notice gigantic spots of water damage forming. Every step I take I must be slow and cautious to prevent falling through the water-logged floors.

Much of the top floor is a mess of ceiling tiles and broken glass.

The auditorium is a true blast from the past. The original seats are completely intact with the only damage being rust formed on their sides. The original velvet curtain hangs elegantly, pulled back as if to present one final show. Lining the stage is an intricate design etched into the stone; the detail is unreal. Thousands of kids would have enjoyed assemblies and performances over the years in this auditorium. This was once the centerpiece of a bustling elementary school, but now sits permanently dormant at the hands of a struggling and desperate city.

The heavy velvet curtain still hangs proudly.

11

M. M. ROSE

When you talk about schools with history in Detroit, one major school comes to mind. M. M. Rose is one of the oldest schools in Detroit and has some serious history involved. It's a miracle it was even standing for me to document the inside. The original single-story school house could be dated back to 1886. It finally received a second story in 1889, despite construction being halted for much of that year. In 1980 the school closed, and all its students were transferred to a newer and more modern school just down the street. Rose was left to rot in the elements. Even the wood boards over the windows look dated and weathered.

The large stone staircase is in fairly good shape for its age.

Creeping through the basement of this school, I am terrified. There are no windows on this level, so I am left to use my flashlight to shine through the dust and darkness. Ducking beneath broken beams and vents, I finally make my way to the stairs. Climbing up the narrow wooden staircase, I finally start to notice the age of this structure. The wood floors creak beneath my feet and I can feel the boards shifting as I walk. The plaster on almost every wall has fallen off, exposing the decaying brick and stone behind it. Every door is warping from the weather and they hardly sit on their hinges anymore.

Old wooden doors that have since taken a beating.

Storage closets for books and class materials inside of this classroom.

In each of the classrooms hangs a special fluorescent light fixture unlike anything I have ever laid eyes on. Four light tubes protrude out of the base of the fixture in a horseshoe shape. I would have loved to see how these things looked while the school was still operational. I am honestly so surprised these lasted this long without damage. Even with the room falling apart, much of the glass on the light fixtures is still completely intact. There is also a lack of graffiti and vandalism in this building. Generally, I find tags and paint covering most of the walls, but in Rose it is just not the case.

A fully intact tube lamp inside of a classroom.

Peeking into the hallway, I cannot believe my eyes. What I see in front of me is absolute destruction. The entire center of the school is collapsed from the roof to the basement. Sunlight peers in from above, illuminating the mangled mess I'm looking down upon. As I approach the center, I must be extremely cautious. I brace myself on the wall as I get in closer to get some photos. It's like a tidal wave of wood and metal frozen in time. It's incredible that this building can withstand so much damage and weathering, but remain relatively undisturbed. It's a true testament to the hard work and time that was put into constructing this school.

Multiple spots of damage can be seen on the floors of the upper levels.

Multiple stories of destruction directly in the center of the school.

A nice view of the mangled mess of this school.

12

RUDDIMAN JR. HIGH SCHOOL

I t's not uncommon for an abandoned school in Detroit to make the news for all the wrong reasons. Often these structures are used for some very illegal activities such as selling drugs, using drugs, or even arson. This idea paints a very negative picture of these buildings and they're usually condemned and locked down to prevent further crime. Unfortunately for Ruddiman Jr. High, something even worse happened behind its closed doors. In 2013, a decapitated body was found inside the vacant school. The body was so decayed that the police were unable to identify the victim. This event really changed the way the neighborhood viewed this building as well as other local schools and spots of abandonment.

Lockers have been overturned and ripped from their original mounted locations.

Even with the new-found knowledge of what had happened inside Ruddiman, I still decided it was important to document its history. As I approach the building, I notice how much space the school occupies. From the outside I can tell this school has a very confusing floor plan and towers over the adjacent roads. Sounds of children playing can be heard all around in the surrounding park. Do they know the dark history about this school? Surely no parent would let their children play outside if they had known, right?

As I push through the side door I am immediately greeted with the most vivid graffiti. Every single surface is coated from the floor to the ceiling. A large open room is coated on all sides with various tags and painted images. The halls are also painted thoroughly and even the stairwells have artists' tags up and down them. Slim rays of light pierce through the security shutters and leave this school feeling uncomfortably ominous. Each stairwell has its own unique style, and makes it confusing to traverse to the upper floors. My skin crawls with the thought of finding something horrendous with each turn I take.

A cafeteria room with a shallow stage on the back wall.

Bright blue paint coats one of the smaller staircases.

Handrails have been removed from this stairwell.

The gym is a disaster and the warped floors make it a challenge to cross. Debris and garbage scatter the floor on all sides. Years of graffiti decorate the walls and even the basketball nets. The auditorium has a very similar theme. The original wood seats remain but are covered with hundreds of fallen ceiling tiles. Remnants of a tattered, royal blue curtain still drape over the narrow stage. The library is a sad shell of what was once something extremely beautiful. The wooden bookshelves are the only thing standing behind a sea of glass. It's only a matter of time before this structure is ultimately leveled and completely forgotten. I am grateful I can see all the beauty the school has to offer and cherish the opportunity to see these dark hallways.

Waves several feet high stretching across the gym floor.

The school auditorium with all its seats in good condition.

Empty bookshelves inside of the school library.

13

SOUTH WESTERN HIGH SCHOOL

The old schools I visit are sometimes very maze-like in their architecture, with each floor twisting and turning in every direction and staircases scattered throughout. To the students who attended these schools, it's second nature to walk those halls, but for an explorer it can be quite the challenge. Intricate hallways were a staple of older schools and learning the floor plan is all part of the fun of the explore. The first time I visited Southwestern High School I found myself finding dead ends and looping hallways quite a bit. To accommodate such a large number of students, the school had quite an expansive hallway system.

A passageway that once led to the main staircase is now busted open.

Entering from the side, I am immediately surprised by the string lights that are turned on through the halls. Long strips of construction lights provide faint light onto the brightly colored yellow lockers. The old tile has been since stripped out as well as the drop ceiling. The empty halls are a faint reminder of what this beautiful relic of history was once like. The tunnel leading from one side of the school to the other has now been stripped of its walls, leaving only the roof and supports.

These lights were put up by the crew that was renovating the inside of this school.

This tunnel connecting one side of the school to the other no longer has walls to protect it from the elements.

I notice certain rooms have more stuff left than others. Some of the rooms have piles of junk swept into one corner, but most have been completely gutted and have no distinct features other than wood shelves and cabinets. It appeared work was being done to transition this school into some sort of industrial offices or lofts. It's unclear when the project is planned to be finished, but the school is in rough shape.

Heavy work benches were left behind from this shop class.

The pool room is iconic in this school. Looking around, all I can notice is the amazing graffiti on the walls. Each wall is decorated in a different design and logo. Brightly colored spray paint coats the inside of the pool as well as on the floor around it. It's clear these artists are very passionate about their work.

The pool room decorated in vivid graffiti.

The auditorium is absolutely heart breaking. There had been a very large fire and it had damaged almost every inch of the room. The stage has begun to crumble to char and the paint peels off the walls in huge sheets. The ornate ceiling can still be seen through the charring, and intricate arches span from one side to the other. Even after the fire, this auditorium kept its charm and beauty. A large tag of graffiti proudly sits on the wall behind the stage.

Opposite above: A grand auditorium severely damaged by fire.

Opposite below: A view from the second-story balcony down onto the burned stage.

14

ST. LUKE CATHOLIC SCHOOL

It's always a sad experience finding people's belongings inside of a building completely forgotten. It's especially sad when you find children's toys or items that can easily be utilized by others. So often I find myself running into rooms full of toys and books and education materials and it's an awful feeling. So much is just wasted while schools in the surrounding areas are struggling to get by. Desks, chairs, books, and other school supplies are some of the most commonly found items inside of abandoned schools. Most of the stuff is in perfect condition and it really makes you wonder why it was left in the first place.

This was a religious school and has religious decorations throughout classrooms.

Walking in through the front doors of the school, I am immediately greeted by a large and dark gymnasium. It appears a fire has ripped through this place, leaving much of it covered in soot and char. It's unfortunately too dark to document. I notice both sides of the gym are lined with tables and other equipment from the cafeteria. It doesn't look like much has been removed since the closing of the school. Under the stage, I notice something quickly scurries from one side to the other. Leaning down, I notice something very peculiar. A cat and her kittens are tucked away in the corner peacefully napping away, true creatures of decay.

Several tube monitors left behind on a teacher's desk.

Each classroom I walk through has more stuff than the last. Children's school toys are tossed all over the floor, creating a sea of color. In every room, I find bookshelves still packed with every single book on display. A few computers are even left sitting on the teachers' desks and throughout what appears to be the computer lab. A large tube TV still sits in one of the classrooms—it's surprising the glass hasn't been shattered. The desks are still lined up in their original formation, each one coated in a thick layer of dust. Even the teachers' desks have lesson plans and class material left behind. Sadly, the final lesson has already been taught.

Opposite above: A child's dusty, stuffed rabbit, forgotten about in a classroom.

Opposite below: A large tube TV in a children's play room.

The common theme of this school appears to be waste. Behind each classroom door there is a cry for help. Every piece of furniture and every book is discarded and forgotten about. The reason why the doors closed is unknown and from my research very little was found about this school. As I walk through the hallways, I truly question why it was left in this shape. Cobwebs hang from the lights and plaster has begun to crack from the brightly colored walls. It truly captures what life was like just before the doors were closed for the last time.

Above: Hundreds of textbooks left behind in the schools' book storage

Opposite above: An old tube monitor with a shelf of children's books.

Opposite below: A stack of discarded American history books.

PLASTIC COMBS
Reading Laboratory 1c
Reading Laboratory 1a

15

VON STEUBEN ELEMENTARY SCHOOL

Constantly seeing beautiful facades and intricate interior features being destroyed or neglected is one of the worst parts of urban exploring. I feel it's very important for me to show off and document these features before they're ultimately forgotten about or demolished. It's uncommon to see much detail or craftsmanship put into modern-day schools so it's always a treat to uncover some architectural masterpiece that I've never visited before. Von Steuben Elementary was certainly a diamond in the rough. The amount of detail in the exterior and interior was incredible, and to my surprise, entirely intact.

An open gym decorated in warmer colors.

Approaching the front of the school I immediately notice the historic façade I'm use to in Detroit schools: big bold windows surrounded by delicate stonework and engraved brick. Even the outside appears to be kept up on, and the walls and sidewalk are mostly clean. From above the overgrown trees and shrubs I can see the signature powerhouse smoke stack proudly towering over the school.

A sign was hung to remind students to not drink contaminated water from the bathroom sinks.

The floors are abnormally clean. I take a second look down as my boots squeak against the tile below. It's not every day I get to explore a school this clean. The lights in the hall still hang, but trying the light switch proves the electricity has been turned off years ago. Lockers are mostly slammed shut and the only things that remain inside are various stickers and papers from past students. Even the hallway clocks still hang; usually these are the first to come down.

Opposite above: The main hallway on the upper floor presenting a line of open classroom doors.

Opposite below: Floors kept squeaky clean even through the school's vacancy.

Everything is built with such detail and the auditorium really showcases the beauty of this school. The wood seats are in excellent condition and glisten from the sunlight. The floors appear to almost have a fresh wax applied, although surely this couldn't be the case. The original forest green curtain is hanging on the stage surrounding the podium, and the multi-colored stage lights can be seen directly above. Unfortunately, there will be no assembly any time soon.

Above: A look at the auditorium seating area from center stage.

Opposite above: Reflective tiled floors in the auditorium.

Opposite below: The green curtain still hangs proudly on stage.

The classrooms are hit the worst from sitting idle for so long. Due to the floors being made from wood, they have transformed into long waves of twisting planks. Most of the chalkboards still have lesson plans scribbled across them. With all the doors closed, it's almost as if the school has only been dormant for a few days.

Opposite above: An American flag hangs above a rippled wooden floor.

Opposite below: A book storage room beginning to take on mold and water damage.

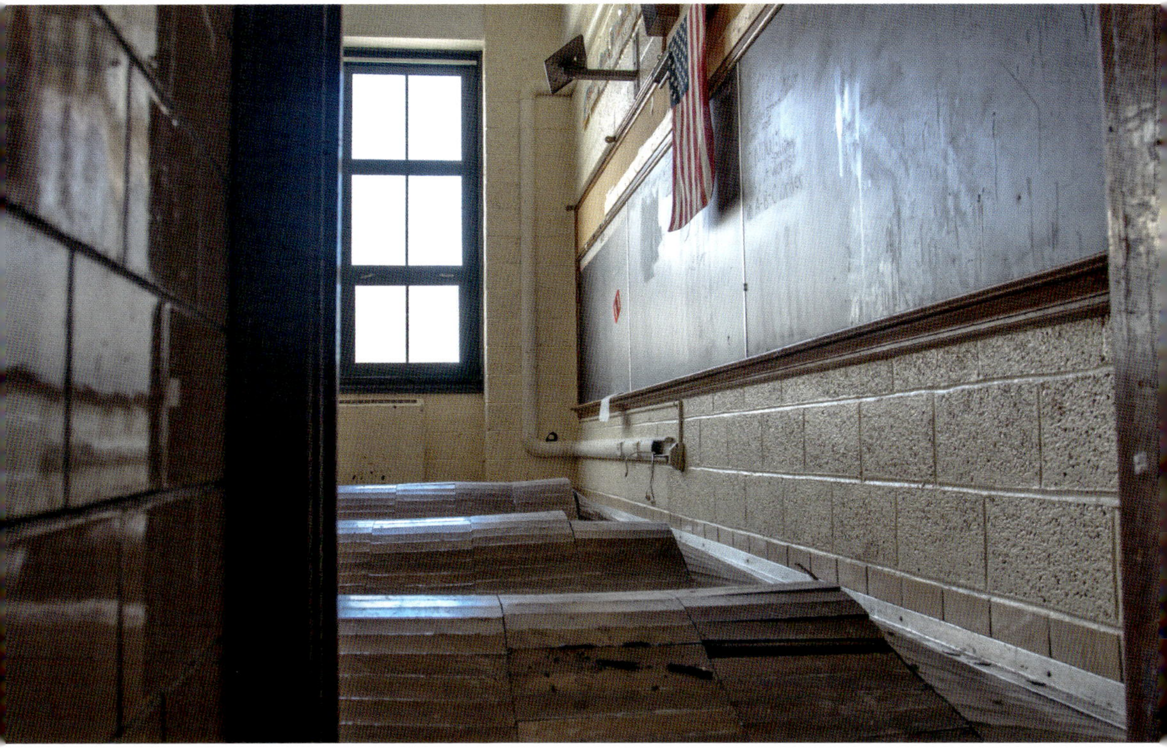

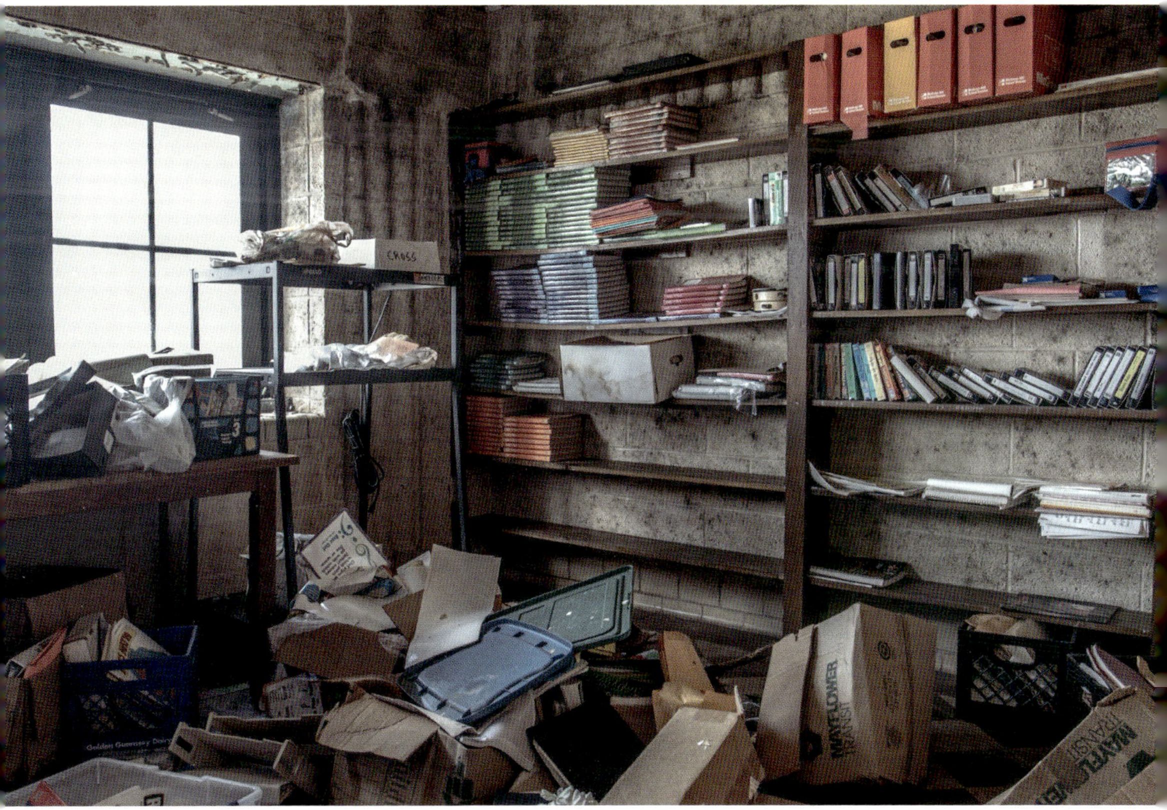
CROSS
MAYFLOWER TRANSIT

American flags can be found still propped up in the classrooms, as if to signify perseverance through decay. This building has stood the test of time for this long with little to no signs of aging. Neglect and weathering takes its course, but the building still stands stronger than ever. Eventually, the building will stand as a husk of something that was once stunning, and its walls will tell a powerful story of depression and corruption. I am always honored to document these buildings and will continue to do so for as long as I am capable.